To Xavier —
You teen hearts
right side up!

[signature]
June 14, 2008
Grant's Farm

Poems, Fables & Sketches

by Byron von Rosenberg:

NMOD

SIDE

UP

THINKing

Thinking Upside Down
Copyright ©2005 Byron von Rosenberg
All rights reserved

Cover Design by Pine Hill Graphics and Red Mountain Creations
Interior Design by Pine Hill Graphics

Packaged by Pine Hill Graphics
85334 Lorane Hwy.
Eugene, OR 97405
www.pinehillgraphics.com

Library of Congress Cataloging-in-Publication Data
(Provided by Cassidy Cataloguing Services, Inc.)

von Rosenberg, Byron.

    Thinking upside down : poems, fables & sketches / by Byron von
    Rosenberg. — 1st ed. — High Ridge, MO : Red Mountain Creations,
    2005.

        p. ; cm.

        ISBN-13: 0-978-0-9759858-2-3
        ISBN-10: 0-9759858-2-5

        1. American poetry. 2. Fables, American. I. Title.

PS3622.O67 T55 2005
811.6—dc22   0509

Printed in the United States of America.

To
Ryan and Erin
Who turned our house upside down
and our hearts right side up!

Red Mountain Creations
P.O. Box 172
High Ridge, MO 63049
Toll Free: 1-866-SEA-GULS
www.byronvonrosenberg.com

Table of Contents

WATCH THE BAT

If you see a little bat
Fly across your page — like that! —
Follow where it's leading
For the poem you are reading
Goes around the bend
Before it makes its end.
(To clarify for my brother Clyde
It continues on the other side!)

THINKING UPSIDE DOWN

I had a dream this morning
And I think I was a bat
'Cause I was hanging upside down!
How can they think like that?
"Keep your feet off of the ceiling!"
That's what my mother said.
"If you put your feet up
Your blood all rushes to your head!"

So how is it that mother bats
Have this lesson switched about?
For when you think upside down
It creates odd looks and doubt!
We say that bats are batty,
Their flight so u n p r e d i c t a b l e.
It's names like that we people use
To make other's thoughts Constrictable.

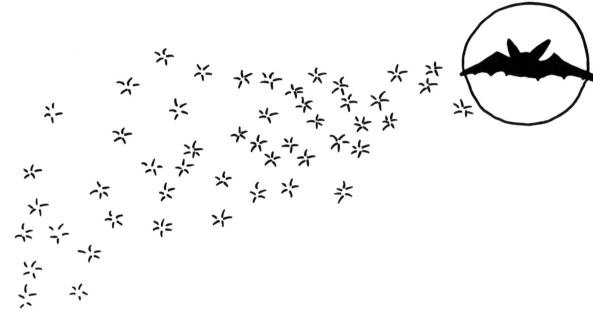

Yet a bat can catch ten thousand bugs
And I can't swat a fly,
And if I'm thinking for myself
I can figure out just why.

Yes, anyone who's different
Is called a freak or clown,
But sometimes great advancements come
From thinking upside down!

THE OTTER OUGHTER

The otter oughter work!
It plays just way too much.
It oughter spend its time
Doing chores and such.
The otter oughter wipe that smile
Right off its silly face,
Get with all the other rats
And live life like a race!
The otter oughter schedule
And organize its time.
Such idleness is sinful!
Why, it's almost a crime!
The otter oughter get a job,
Keep its money in a bank.
When it makes these changes
It will have me to thank!
Odd the otter knows
The best in life is free.
The otter oughter teach
That lesson now to me!

ARNOT AND ARTU, THE LLAMAS FROM FRANCE

Arnot and Artu were llamas from France
Who couldn't agree on their cans and their can'ts.
Arnot would say "No" to his sister Artu
Who ended up taking the opposite view.
The subject in question never did matter
And their arguments ended in spit and in splatter
Until on the day Arnot realized
If he'd agree with his sister they'd both be surprised.
Artu was amazed and responded in kind
And if you'd do the same I think that you'd find
That the people who love you are worth taking that chance
Like Arnot and Artu, the llamas from France.

SUPER-FROG

He could leap over the dog house.
It took just a single bound!
He hopped faster than a rabbit
And he sure could cover ground.
He could snap his tongue and catch a bug
Twenty feet away
And any kid who picked him up
Was repelled by his awesome spray.
He was the biggest strongest frog
The planet's ever seen.
His amphibious friends all envied him.
(That's why they're all still green.)
He didn't have a thing to prove
For his fame was widely known
But he wanted to stop a train like Superman
To show how strong he'd grown.
He hopped down to the station
To catch the nine o'clock.
He waited across the street
To show off for his webbed-foot flock.
When the nine o'clock came rolling in
He jumped high across the road
But not high enough to miss my car...

14

And I squashed him like a toad!

Super-Frog, oh, Super-Frog!
Why did it have to end like that?
In his epic last performance
Super-Frog seemed a little flat!

15

I'M COLLECTING

I'm collecting calendars
And I want yours today
So you can spend some time with me
And we can laugh and play.

I'm collecting smiles
From all the folks I know
So if you have one locked inside
Could you please let it go?

I'm collecting compliments.
I have one hundred eighty-two.
That's more than I could ever use
So I'll give a bunch to you.

I'm collecting friends.
(I want a lot, you see.)
I'm hoping I can find someone
(Like you!) collecting me!

FREE BALLOONS

I'm giving away free balloons,
Big and fat and round,
Hoping if you take one
My feet will reach the ground!

17

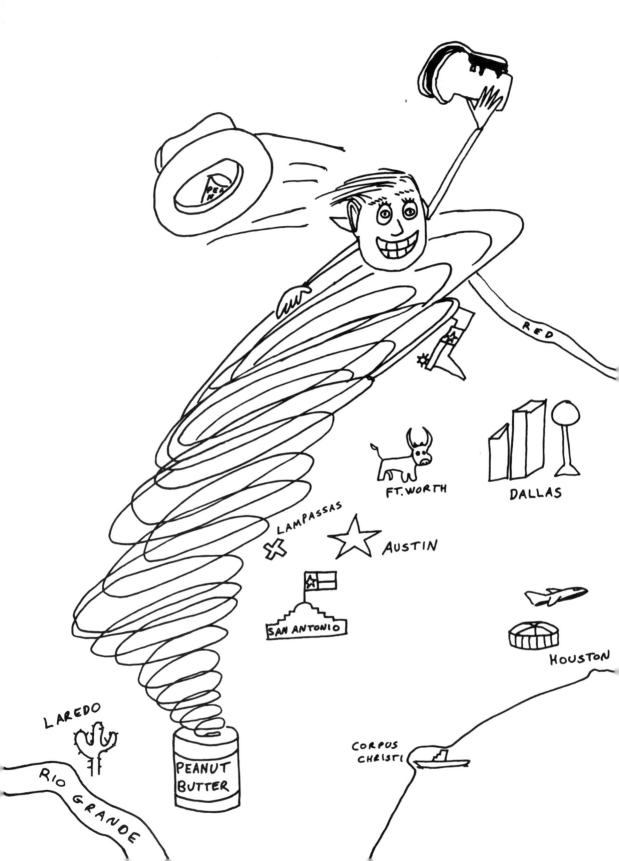

THE BALLAD OF PEANUT BUTTER PETE

He roped a twister like Pecos Bill and rode it in a test of will
Across the entire Lone Star state until the great winds did abate.
They cheered him down in Mexico, "Viva, viva! What a show!
From the Red to the Rio Grande! How, Pete, how?" He held out his hand.
"PBJ," he said with a smile, "helps me hold on quite a while.
On my hand or in my tummy, that's the best, for it's quite yummy!
Straight out of a gallon jar or from a shot glass at the bar!
My momma put it in my soup. It tasted good and cured the croup.
It's the only thing I'll ever eat. Hi! I'm Peanut Butter Pete!"
Across the west his legend grew and he owed it all to that sticky goo.
He ran for sheriff on a bet with a winning phrase they can't forget:
"He'll stick it out through thin and thick. His aim is sure and his draw is quick!
It's peanut butter, not molasses. Vote for Pete here in Lampassas!"
He won two hundred votes to twenty and brought in PBJ aplenty.

He kept a stash 'most everywhere — in his desk, beside his chair,
'Neath the saddle of his horse (just to hold it on, of course).
Never once did he admit, "It's PB's fault my pants don't fit!"
It filled the holster of his gun and in a duel he was undone
For his pistol stuck and wouldn't fire. He was bleedin' bad, his chances dire.
"Doc," he said, "give it to me straight." "You're gonna die, Pete, it's much too late."
"Not too late!" they heard him utter. "Bring me all my peanut butter!"
He ate and ate, then they heard him roar, "I'm feeling better! Bring me more!"
They brought it out in gallons and tubs and lathered him with massages and rubs.
And then the tearful eyes were dry as they heard the doctor's cheerful cry.
"Glory be! God rest my soul! The PBJ's filled up the hole!"
He wobbled slowly to his feet and ambled gamely down the street.
He lived to see another day, thanks in full to PBJ.
Now here's the jelly, here's the bread. Lay on thick that glorious spread!
And now pretend you're PB Pete. It's lunchtime, kid. Sit down and eat!

PROPHET THE LLAMA

Prophet the Llama was split half and half.
It turned people's heads and made most of them laugh.
He always stood rigid. He never did sway
And no one could ever find one hair of gray.
He was black on one side and white on the other,
A fact that perturbed his father and mother
For he wasn't like them to go along with the herd.
If he saw it that way, he'd call it absurd.
He didn't have many friends for being so curt
For llamas, like people, get their feelings hurt.

But when they had to decide which way to go
The llamas all knew that Prophet would know.
He'd tell them the truth (he never did fail)
And point right or left with his two-colored tail.
I've known people like Prophet who never blink.
They look ordinary but, in truth, are distinct.
For truth is a commodity sacred and rare
That shows in your heart much more than your hair.
In the face of a lie, can you say what is true?
Then you'll stand out like Prophet and we'll all look to you.

OOKLE MCGOOKLE

Ookle McGlookle, that magnificent ape,
Flew through the air in top-hat and cape!
On Saturday evening he went into town,
He in his top-hat, his wife in her gown.
But some people laughed and sneered at the sight
While others screamed and ran off in fright!
It hurt Ookle so to be treated this way
And he hasn't returned to this very day.
He's probably out there, high up in a tree
Where we people think a monkey should be.
And I think of Ookle, that lost, lonely ape,
Whenever I try to, but cannot escape.

LEAP FROM YOUR DREAMS

It seems like I am stuck
In my dreams 'most all the time.
I just can't get out.
It's too hard a climb.
This morning I decided
I would finally escape
And swing out of my dreams
On the backside of an ape!
It swung high and low
And touched 'most every tree,
But it had no real direction
and was of no help to me.
I got a ride upon a hippo.
Now that was quite a blunder!
I couldn't get a grip
And kept on sliding under!
And then it got much worse.
It swam into the lake!
Whatever you may do,
Please don't make my mistake.

23

Next I tried an antelope.
Boy, do they run fast!
But it would never stop!
It kept on going past.
All the places I would see
Were gone in just a blink.
I'd like to slow it down a bit
And enjoy my life, I think!
Now the next thing that I did
Might appeal somewhat to you.
I got inside the pouch
Of a giant kangaroo!
But it was way to bumpy
With the starting and the stopping.
To get out of my dreams
Will take much more than hopping.

And in sadness I looked down
And there were my two feet,
A pair to call my own.
Hey! That's pretty neat!
They're not built as are an ape's
To grab onto a vine.
They're not giant like a hippo's
But the good thing is — they're mine!
They can't keep up with an antelope
Or hop like that big 'roo,

But to leap out of my dreams
Just this pair alone will do.
So I thanked all of the animals
For the kindness they had shown
Then leapt out of my dreams
With those two feet of my own!
Yes, now you know the secret
And you're well on your way,
So leap out of your dreams
And into this great day!

25

THE LITTLE PYROMANIAC

He could always start a campfire
With just a match or two,
And flames would climb to twenty feet
Before that lad was through.
His father warned him many times
That fire was really hot,
But like too many boys these days
Listen, he would not.
He found a can of gasoline
High on a shelf, well hidden.
Got a ladder, brought it down,
Though he knew it was forbidden.
He took it to the outhouse;
Poured it down the pit.
"Eliminate the smell," he thought,
"That'll be the end of it."

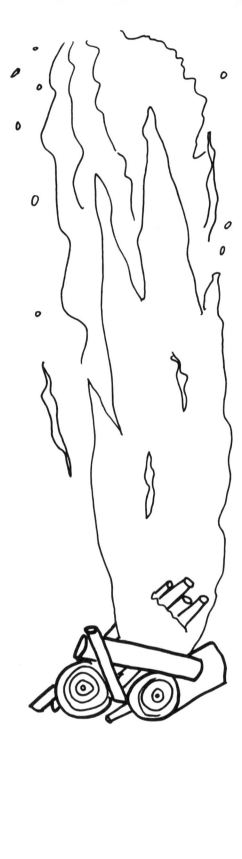

But when he tossed the match
The entire outhouse blew!
It layered all the field
And the little pyro, too.
Yes, he raised a stink that day,
One skill that he could master.
Follow rules! Don't play with fire!
Or you court your own disaster.

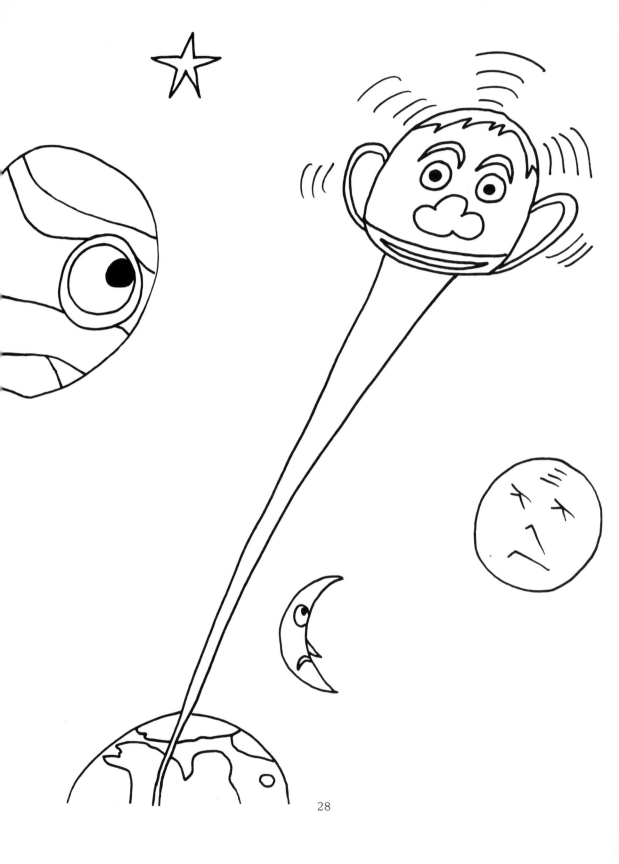

OLLIE, THE BOBBLE-HEAD BOY

Oliver, the Bobble-head boy,
Was never happy as a toy.
Wanted legs and feet to walk
And especially a tongue to talk.
A nearby fairy heard his wish.
Granted! (With a wandly swish!)
"Just one thing that you should know:
Tell a lie, your neck will grow!"
Ollie nodded (as he always did)
But let the lies flow from his lid.
Big ones! Small ones! So he grew
And told some more to birds that flew.
Reached up to a satellite;
Was on a TV show last night!
He told so many! Grew so fast!
He reached up to the moon and past!
On to Mars and Jupiter
Went the bobble Oliver.
No one talks to Ollie now.
(Those who want to don't know how!)
He tells his lies in outer space
But here or there it's still disgrace.
The consequences are no cure
Else we'd all tell the truth for sure!
(If from this tale you did not discern
This last line means SOME FOLKS DON'T LEARN!)

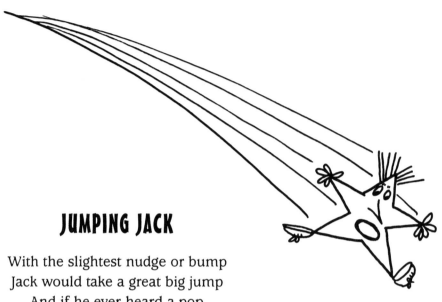

JUMPING JACK

With the slightest nudge or bump
Jack would take a great big jump
And if he ever heard a pop
You'd be amazed how high he'd hop!
When his dog surprised him with a nip
Jack jumped and did a triple flip.
So hold your breath around him, please!
He'd jump a mile with just a sneeze.
Oops! Too late! I heard a beep!
I wonder where old Jack did leap.
Out in space, if I know Jack.
Jumped so high he can't come back.
So when I see a shooting star
I'll wave and call, "Jack! There you are!"

THE FLIGHT OF THE SUPER-FROG

Oh, how that frog could hop!
No creature jumped as high
But Super-Frog would not be satisfied.
He was determined he would fly!
He watched the fireworks show
And the bottle rockets soar.
If he could just ride one of those
He'd be the stuff of ancient lore!
He waited for a big one,
Hopped on when it was lit.
What a view of earth he'd have
When up in space he'd sit!
Hanging on that comet
He flew a fiery arc,
And Super-Frog lit the sky that night
As he spread across the dark.

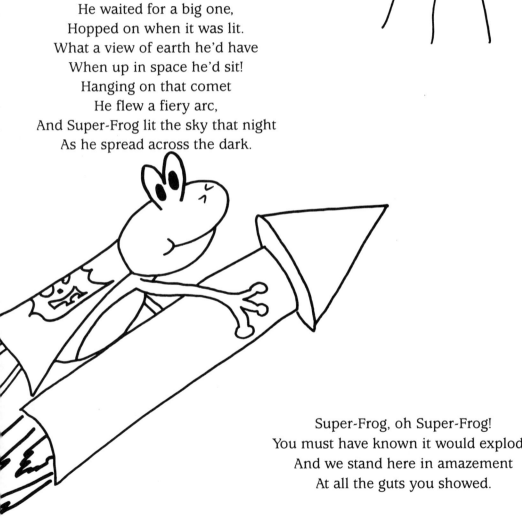

Super-Frog, oh Super-Frog!
You must have known it would explode,
And we stand here in amazement
At all the guts you showed.

31

WALTER WUPPERMAN'S WINGS

They gathered along Texas Street
From top to bottom of the hill,
And as Walter stepped out from the walk
The crowd was hushed and still.
He was tall and skinny for his age
With arms especially long.
He had flapped his wings for weeks
To try to make them strong.
The bruises were still visible
From his last aborted goof,
But his cardboard wings had padded him
When he jumped off of the roof.

His wingspan was impressive
As he turned into the wind,
And the crowd all held its breath
As he started to descend.
Walter took those giant strides
And flapped with all his might.
If trying could have given lift
He would have taken flight.
When Walter reached the bottom
His arms were tired and sore,
And his mother seemed relieved
When he said, "I'll try no more!"
But everyone who watched him
Has remembered to this day
The time that Walter Wupperman
Tried to fly away.

INVASION OF THE WOODPECKERS

I listened to the woodpecker
As it knocked upon the tree.
Knowing that it ate parasites
Was comforting to me.
I was delighted when two of them
Flew over from next door
But did not know what to do
When I saw a hundred more.
The sky was dark with woodpeckers.
The trees were shaking with their blows!
By spring these ravaged trees would die
For with such damage nothing grows.
The woodpeckers kept on pecking
After all the bugs and bark were gone.
They kept on sinking holes all night
And there were more of them by dawn!
The invasion of the woodpeckers
Is an awesome, dreadful sight
And the next time you stop to criticize,
Remember it you might.

CLIMB THE RED MOUNTAIN

Only for an instant
Late in the waning year,
Only one place to see it
And I am standing here.
The leaves have turned from green
To orange, yellow, and brown,
And are red only on the mountain
Just as the sun goes down.
Beautiful beyond belief,
I am the only one who sees it!
This chance may come but a single time;
I must act now to seize it!
Climb the crimson mountain slopes
As the sun sinks low in the sky!
What will you find when you reach the top?
You won't know unless you try!

TURNABOUT MOUNTAIN

"You've come far," the old man said,
"I'd even say done well.
But the final outcome's yet to be
And what comes next will tell.
Cast your eyes into the sunset,
To that highest mountain peak,
For unless you reach the top
You'll never gather what you seek.
Many have tried to pass that way,
So many I quit countin',
But most I see head back this way
When they come to
Turnabout Mountain."

The old man shook his head,
Admitted, "Yes, I too once tried.
I almost made it to the top
But then the oxen died.
A blizzard came howling from the north
With twenty feet of snow.
Least that's how I remember it,
'Twas so long ago.
I'd go with you once again
If it weren't for all this doubtin'.
Afraid that's the thing that happens
When you turn back at
Turnabout Mountain."

The old man turned about
And peered into the west.
I think he must have wondered
If in truth he'd done his best.
But his words deepened our resolve
That we would not be broken.
We made a promise with our eyes
Though not a word was spoken.
For such a fellowship as ours
There can be no accountin'.
It's all for one and one for all
To conquer Turnabout Mountain.

The blizzards came, the oxen died,
But we climbed while we had breath,
For our resolve was "it or us"!
We were in it to the death.
Each step was utter agony
But it felt worse to stop
And because we climbed together
We each made it to the top.
The dreams we had came true
With blessings like a fountain!
That's what happens when you stick it out
In spite of Turnabout Mountain.

That was many years ago
And now I too am old.
All are gone who climbed with me
And made that trip so bold.
Yet they live on in me
And we'll live on in you,
For when you see that distant peak
We know what you will do.
Like us you'll brave the danger
And we'll know it from the shoutin',
That you have made it to the top
And over Turnabout Mountain.

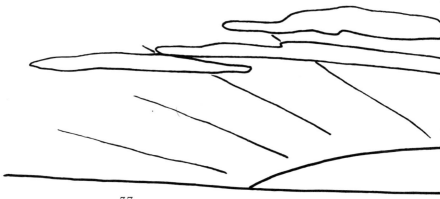

ENDGAME

A king, a castle,
Just one pawn,
The queen, her court,
Long since gone.
Alone these face
The fierce onslaught,
One last battle,
So many fought.

There is no rest
Through struggles long.
Fatigued and weary,
They must be strong.
All that's happened
Heretofore
For naught unless
They win one more.
On my mind
This game depends
And I'll be standing
When it ends.

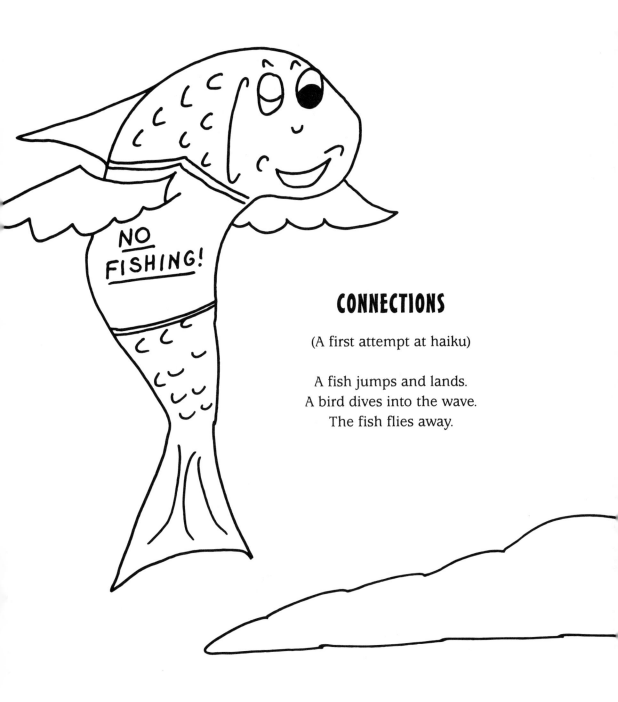

CONNECTIONS

(A first attempt at haiku)

A fish jumps and lands.
A bird dives into the wave.
The fish flies away.

IVAN THE TERRIER

A little bark, a tiny dog,
No bigger than a minute,
But play a game of tug-o-war
And that dog thinks he'll win it!
I lift the rope and there he hangs,
Rope clenched between his jaws.
He spins and wriggles in the air
Madly waving all four paws.
I set him down to see
If he'll finally give it up,
But he thinks he's winning now.
I'll have to show that pup!
I take the rope away,
Say, "NO! That's it!"
But though I think it's over
Ivan simply will not quit.
It's always the persistent one
Who wins our backyard game,
And if you don't give up your dreams
You'll find that life is just the same.
He's the smallest dog in any hunt
But his spirit knows no barrier.
Want to win against all odds?
Watch Ivan, the tenacious terrier!

IVAN THE TERRIER'S TAIL

Look at Ivan the terrier!
The dog has lost his tail!
We thought it might grow back
But hoped to no avail.
We called the man we bought him from.
He said to call the vet's
Who told us that his tail was gone
And one is all he gets.
What do they do with puppy tails
They've whacked off with a knife?
Ivan doesn't think of such;
He goes on with his life.
He wags the stub that he has left;
He runs around and plays.
Life's shorter than a terrier's tail
So be happy all your days.
Things that can't be changed,
Don't let them plague your mind,
Amazing things that we can learn
From a terrier's behind!

OIL AND WATER

"That new kitten's ears
Seem so very long
And its meow sounds like a growl!
I hope that nothing's wrong.
It likes to chase a ball
And sometimes to chase me
But that nose is just too huge!
I wonder, can it see?
Perhaps it's feeling lonely
For it really is quite strange.
Maybe if I play with it
Its mood would start to change."

"That's the oddest puppy
That I have ever known.
I've seen dogs with spots before
But not the stripes it's grown!
I've never heard it bark,
Just a whimper now and then,
And it really does smell different.
I wonder where its been!
I suppose if I can just look past
Its idiosyncrasies,
It could be my friend
As long as there's no fleas!"

The kitten and the puppy dog
Have formed an odd alliance
For oil and water do not mix.
(I learned that in science!)
What one sees in the other
Is what happens in return,
A lesson from two baby pets
That we all ought to learn.
I watch them romp and run,
See how happily they play,
And wish there were more people
Who saw the world that way.

TREED OFF

I don't think she'd ever been outside.
(It's a place she never goes.)
But there she was high in a tree!
How she got there no one knows.
That cat was wailing wildly.
It broke my heart to hear her cry.
Before I called the firemen
I thought I'd give it one good try.
I went and got a ladder,
Set it up against the tree,
Whispered softly to the cat,
"Don't worry now, it's me."
But the cat who'd warmed my lap
On many a winter's night
Somehow saw a snarling bear
And clawed at me in fright.
I drew my hand back quickly
But it was badly tattered!
I lost my balance, grabbed a branch,
For I was now unladdered.

And now just like the frightened cat
I could not get down.
The phone was in the house
And 'twas an hour's drive from town.
When the firemen finally came
The cat was calm and mellow,
But I was bleeding pretty bad
And my underwear was yellow.
I, too, can laugh about it now
But it surely wasn't fun,
And next time my cat gets in the tree
I'm calling nine-one-one!

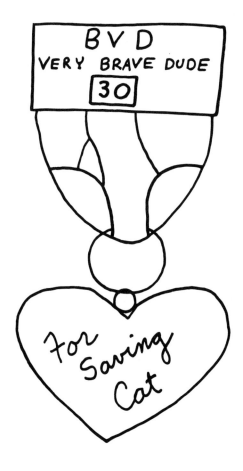

DANCES WITH CATS

She was graceful, agile and spry,
The nimblest of acrobats.
She had such feline grace in the air
They called her "Dances with Cats."
They had a photo shoot at the circus
And five hundred cats filled the room.
"Dances with Cats" started to sneeze
As her allergies sprang into bloom.
She gave a nimble sneeze to her left
And a less graceful one to her right.
She cancelled the evening's performance
And stayed up coughing all night.

Because she couldn't withstand it
She ended up changing her name.
"Sneezes with Cats" has less charm
But her performance is always the same.
She can laugh at her own little failures
(For over some things she has no control)
So when you're facing a tough situation
Remember humor can play a role.
She now lives with five cats in her mansion
That she rescued one day from the pound
And between sneezes she shares a lesson
That through such occurrence she's found.
"Be kind to those who afflict you
(There is a gift for those who do)
For all the good that you do for others
Will double and come back - ACHOO!!"

MY TEACHER IS...

My teacher is a treasure.
My teacher is a saint.
My teacher's glad it's three o'clock
'Cause what she is...

My teacher knows her science.
She knows her 'rithmatic.
She knows when she has had enough,
That's why she...

My teacher loves her students.
My teacher loves this class.
My teacher says she'll go insane
If all of us...

My teacher said she'd miss us.
She said, "Most terribly!"
My teacher got committed
And they threw away...

My teacher knew my name.
My teacher knew my face.
My principal said that when he asked
No one would...

I'm searching on the internet
To find some way to reach her.
Can she talk me out of it?
I want to...

...A TREASURE

...we ain't!

...called in sick!

...don't pass!

...the key!

...take her place!

...be a teacher!

THE GINGERBREAD MAN GETS A HAIRCUT

He asked me if I'd use my teeth
To trim it just a touch,
But he kind of lost his head
When I bit off way too much.
For when it comes to cutting hair
I haven't got a clue
So get down to the barbershop
And be glad it wasn't you!

THE DEAD SNAKE'S BITE

He dug it up. He had to see.
He found the severed head.
He touched it unafraid
For it was clearly dead.
He laughed to think how scared he was
When he heard its rattle near,
And put his finger in its mouth
To prove he had no fear.
He felt his heartbeat quicken
Though the snake could not attack.
He imagined it alive again
And drew his finger quickly back.

Alas! He touched the hanging tooth!
His finger snagged and bled.
He felt the venom's vicious gnaw
And then in fear, he fled.

Though you win the battle,
Taunting's never right.
When you dig up buried dangers
Expect the dead snake's bite!

THE BREATH HOLDING CONTEST

Just three feet of water,
Pretty hard to drown!
Who would need a breath first
And who would be the last one down?
Some came up in thirty seconds,
Most in just a minute,
And fifteen seconds later
Only two could win it.
They fought fire in their lungs
To a minute forty-five,
Then one came up for air
While the other took a dive.

They quickly pulled him out
And laid him on the dock.
The lifeguards gave him CPR
While the crowd all watched in shock.
Their turn now to choke a breath
'Til he inhaled again,
And almost instantly he asked,
"Tell me, did I win?"
His pride had got the best of him,
A nearly fatal blunder.
Do we learn from our mistakes?
It gives me cause to wonder.

TELEPATHIC TINA

She answers all the telephones
That ring for miles around.
She can tell what folks are thinking
With just the slightest sound!
She can hang up on the salesmen
Before they can solicit
And some things she can't tell you
For they are too explicit!
She can tell who's nice
And naughty just like Santa
So now she makes the lists
For St. Louis and Atlanta.
She knows where you were on Mother's Day
And what you did instead.
It's really disconcerting
That she knows what's in my head!

You should always watch your words
No matter whom you call
And keep your thoughts nice and clean
'Cause Tina knows them all!

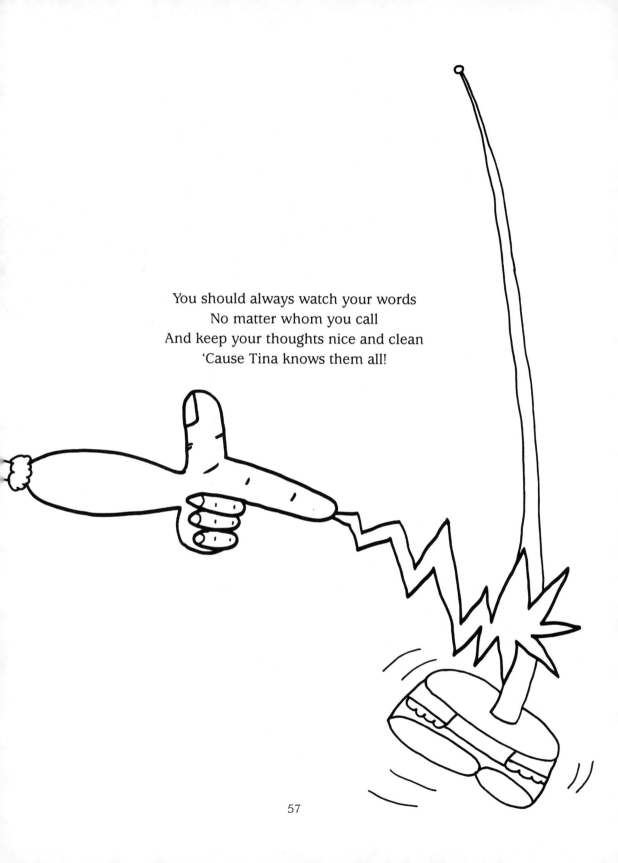

GENE CLEANS

I like it when Gene cleans!
It brightens up my day
For he wipes more than glass
With his rag and spray.
Every cloud is gone
By the time that he is through
And I think that it is Gene
Who puts the sparkle on the dew.
I thank him for his efforts
In shining up the glass
And tell him that his special touch
Allows the light to pass.
He smiles at the happy thought,
Puts his hand upon his chin.
"I can change the weather!"
He tells me with a grin.

"I made it clear today
And the earth shines like a star
But look for rain tomorrow
'Cause I'm gonna wash my car!"

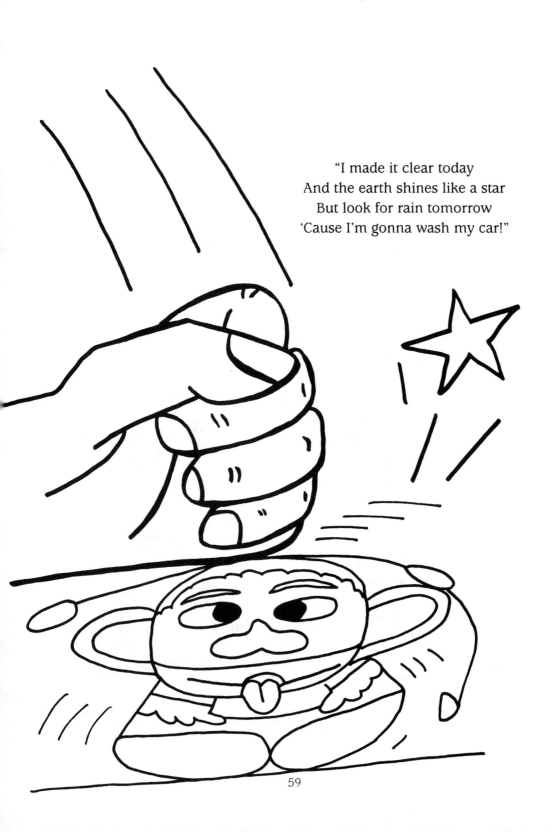

PUDDLES

It takes a lot of effort
To splash the mud all out
But then I get to take it home.
Can't wait to hear Mom shout!
The poet that I am today
Sits around and muddles
But the little boy inside of me
Would rather play in puddles.

ALONZO THE TINKERER

Alonzo likes to tinker with his watches and his clocks
And to make them all run backwards he reversed the ticks and tocks.
Now the sun sets in the east and June follows July.
The astronomers are all confused since he turned back the sky.
A calendar for next year you will not be needing.
You'd better find the old ones for all the years preceding!
My checks are going to bounce 'cause payday was tomorrow
And my neighbor won't give back the things he came to borrow.
I get farther from the finish line the faster that I run.
Please someone tell Alonzo that's not how things are done!
I liked the way things were before with the tocks after the ticks
So never give Alonzo another clock to fix!

MCMIII

JIM STEMMLER'S FAMOUS ROOT BEER FLOATS

They had to close down Market Street
In front of City Hall.
The line stretched to the Arch and back
And Jimbo served them all.
They had to build a factory
To make enough ice cream!
Jim Stemmler's famous root beer floats,
Far better than a dream!
No one seems to mind
That they have to wait a while.
They plunk down their three dollars
And Jim greets them with a smile.
They say, "Jim, you could be rich
If you did this all the time."
But Jimbo gives it all away!
He never keeps a dime.
"It's how you pour the root beer," says Jim,
"That makes my floats so sweet.
But helping others, those in need,
That's my most special treat."

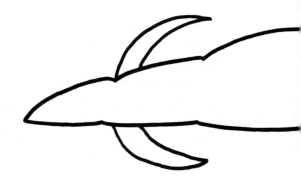

THE PAINTER AND THE POET

The poet sees the painter
correcting his mistakes,
who makes the painting beautiful
in spite of all he makes,
for the painter paints them over
to make his picture true
while the poet points them out
and for that same reason, too.

GLUE

Helps to make a picture,
Holds puzzles in their place.
Sticks two things together,
Puts stars upon your face.
Be loyal to your friends
And always say what's true.
Do the right thing every day
And you won't be needing glue.

COME OUT SMILING

When I first met the man
Old Russ was eighty-three,
And what I remember most
Is how he smiled at me.
We sat across the table
To share the morning's bread.
I asked him what he knew of life
And this is what he said.
"I've traveled all the world
And sailed the seven seas
And people often ask,
'Uncle Russ, what are life's keys?'
And I remember what my mother said
When I was just a boy.
'Russ, you came out smiling.
Meet every day with joy!'
And that is what I've always done
Everywhere I've been.
When joy comes from the heart
You will always win.
So don't bother making lists
Of those facts you are compiling
Just write, 'Every day's a blessing
But you have to come out smiling!'"

KICKING BACK

I packed the donkey with my things
And took it by the lead,
But no amount of prodding
Would move this "noble" steed.
I yelled in anger, swung my stick,
And then in pain for it did kick!
The humiliation was so bitter
But gave me cause to reconsider
Why I do the things I do
And what a donkey's going through.
After all, it's not its stuff!
Maybe half this weight's enough.
So I got myself a second one
And didn't have to prod to run.
I used my head. Now that's a trick
Better than a rod or brick.

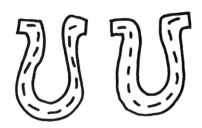

With this knowledge I am wise,
Not a donkey in a man's disguise.
For though two donkeys walk by me
When I use my brain you won't see three.

THE SQUIRRELS' QUARREL

The squirrels quarrel
Over acorns in the fall
As if a single squirrel
Could store and eat them all.
The squirrels quarrel with the birds
When spring comes into season
But why I cannot tell!
They don't seem to need a reason.
The squirrels quarrel all day long
And it makes me laugh a lot
'Cause I like to think I'm different
But you know — I'm really not!

ROSES

Soft and velvet to the touch,
A beauty to the eye,
A fragrance sweetly gentle
With thorns that make you cry.
"Just so much like life,"
The philosopher supposes.
"I can live with thorns
But not without the roses."

MY PET POSSUM

It bites. It fights. It stays up nights.
But I love my pet opossum!
So I'll not revile its teeth or smile
But I'll think before I floss 'em!

THE WITCHES' BREW

As the leaves were turning in the fall
The teacher sternly told us all,
"Write a bit on Halloween,
You with minds so quick and keen!"
I gulped and swallowed. What to do?
I'll write about the witches' brew!

Stir and stir and stir some more,
The stench too much to e'er ignore.
Tail of newt and spider eyes
But a taste of this won't make you wise!
Add a rancid wing of bat!
Don't think you'll be cured by that.
This kind of stew is just no good.
They'd put you in it if they could!
So run away and down the street.
Better stick to trick or treat!
So dress in costume, have your fun!
I'm so glad this poem's done!

OOPS!

When I make a big mistake,
Oh, how my visage droops!
But I have to watch my words
'Cause there are lots of snoops.
The worst things always happen
Before the biggest groups
So I'll practice hard and hope
The worst I say is "Oops!"

MY CELL PHONE

It rings me in the car.
It rings in sun or rain.
It really is convenient,
But today it is a pain!
Every time I get away
My cell phone rings to spoil it.
Even in the bathroom!
And now, deep in the toilet.

CALLING
911

A POSSUM TAIL

A possum tail, a dried up frog,
A stinking yellow snake.
A skin of something with red bugs
I found beside the lake.
I'm gathering together
These fondest memories.
Mom will let me keep them
If I ask her, "Pretty please!"
She's not like my sister
Even though she is a girl.
I don't think she'll mind
When I bring home my squirrel!
Yes, I want to thank my mother
In a very special way
So I'll give her all my treasures
And call it Mother's Day!

KING LOUIE'S HORSE'S BUTT:
A LOVE STORY

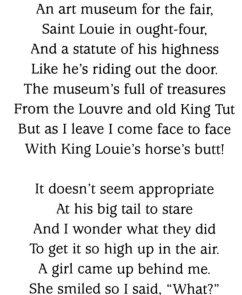

An art museum for the fair,
Saint Louie in ought-four,
And a statute of his highness
Like he's riding out the door.
The museum's full of treasures
From the Louvre and old King Tut
But as I leave I come face to face
With King Louie's horse's butt!

It doesn't seem appropriate
At his big tail to stare
And I wonder what they did
To get it so high up in the air.
A girl came up behind me.
She smiled so I said, "What?"
She said, "I think that yours is cuter
Than King Louie's horse's butt."

I was quite astounded
But I kind of liked the line
And when I got to know her
I vowed to make her mine.
We two think so much alike
As from one stone we're cut
So the two of us got married
Under King Louie's horse's butt!

We still visit the museum
And walk in Forest Park
And at night we hold each other's hands
And kiss there in the dark.
If I tell you where we like to kiss
You'll think that I'm a nut.
We stand in moonlit shadows
Of King Louie's horse's butt!

I know the statute will be there
When we are old and grey
For our love, like that old horse's butt,
Will never go away.
And on our anniversary
Up museum steps I'll strut
To kiss my wife and wave
At King Louie's horse's butt!

I wonder what we look like
From that pedestal above
And where our tale would rank
In the history of love.
But you would be quite lucky
Before life's book is shut
If you could have a love like ours
And King Louie's horse's butt.

THE FLATULENT FLUTIST

Of the stories I've told this one is the cutest
So hear ye the tale of the flatulent flutist.
When he played up an octave he lifted his leg.
"Play only the low notes!" the musicians would beg.
Rat-a-tat-tat was heard in the room.
It wasn't the drum but the flutist's perfume.
All in the orchestra cried as they played!
Crowds ran for the exits. Not a single one stayed.
The air grew dark in the orchestra pit.
For the conductor to see a candle was lit,
And just at that moment came a flatulent toot...

The last and the loudest note played on that flute.

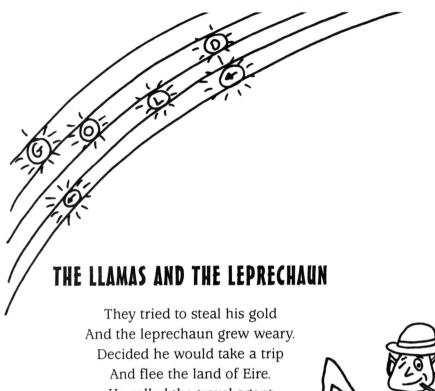

THE LLAMAS AND THE LEPRECHAUN

They tried to steal his gold
And the leprechaun grew weary.
Decided he would take a trip
And flee the land of Eire.
He called the travel agent
To set up his vacation,
But his cell phone didn't work well.
(It had too much vibration.)
"Send me somewhere warm," he said,
"Down to the Bahamas."
But the message they received
Was, "Send me seven llamas!"

82

They came overnight delivery
In a box quite badly splitting,
Soggy, too, from all the phlegm
The angry beasts were spitting.
He phoned his errant agent
To get the thing corrected
But the satellite was crooked
And his message was deflected.
And so he kept the llamas
To protect his golden pot
Since no one else would want one
Smeared with llama snot!
Through this tragic error
He smiled and made the most.
For leprechaun or human
That's not too bad a boast!
The leprechaun had faced his fate
With humor and with pluck.
Do the same and you will find
You'll make your own good luck!

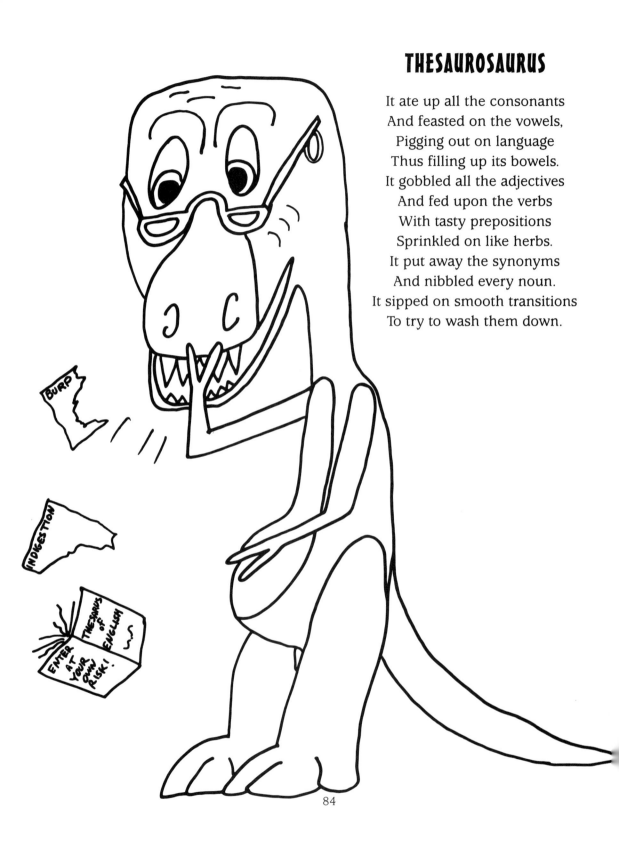

THESAUROSAURUS

It ate up all the consonants
And feasted on the vowels,
Pigging out on language
Thus filling up its bowels.
It gobbled all the adjectives
And fed upon the verbs
With tasty prepositions
Sprinkled on like herbs.
It put away the synonyms
And nibbled every noun.
It sipped on smooth transitions
To try to wash them down.

It gulped and swallowed present,
Past, and future tenses
Committing all conceivable
Devouring offenses.
But it doesn't pay to eat so fast.
It choked on a vernacular!
And the language that spewed forth
Was really quite spectacular!
Yes, a thesaurosuarus's eating habits
Are thoroughly detestable,
But even its great gastric powers
Find English indigestible!

THESE GEESE DON'T FLY ON TUESDAYS

The sun was setting that Tuesday eve
As I neared the mountain top
But even with my lack of time
The scene before me made me stop.
A giant waterfall
Was dammed completely dry.
Geese that should be heading south
Wouldn't flap their wings to fly.
The trail that led to the highest peak
Was blocked by a giant gate.
A sign on the nearby cabin said,
"He who knocks, must wait."
"Hello," I called, "What's happened here?"
"Is everything okay?"
I never saw the man inside
But here's what I heard him say:
"These geese don't fly on Tuesdays!
The fish don't swim after eight.
We never take a chance here!
If we do, we're always late.
The waterfall doesn't run in summer.
We don't harvest grain in fall,
And if we do not water them,
These trees don't grow at all.

We don't have leaves to rake!
We never have grass to mow.
There's nothing that we want to learn!
We know all there is to know.
I won't climb that mountain
And I won't take that trail.
I won't try a thing that's new!
That way I'll never fail."

The woods were strangely silent
And the air was dead to sound.
The flowers that once had bloomed here
Returned to barren ground.
The best thing I could do
Was to leave that man in peace,
But I threw a rock as I climbed the trail
And off flew all the geese.

THE TRAMPOLINE OF LIFE

Up and down and on and off
The backyard trampoline
And I wonder, if I think a bit,
There's a lesson I can glean.
The children bounce each other.
Everyone's affected,
And in the life we lead today
We are "interconnected."
It's funny how the trampoline
Seems to bring two kids together.
Is love merely a happenstance
Or a kind of magic tether?
Some are flipping, shouting out.
Others, silent, sit.
Does what you get in life
Come from what's put into it?
There's a time for action
And there's a time for rest.
You'll need a bit of both
If you're to do your best.

There's bumping with the jumping.
Expect a knock or two!
Playing on the trampoline
Is still so fun to do!
And when someone is called home
It changes how I play.
I'm sad they had to go
But I jump on anyway!
For now it is my turn
To stretch out to the sky,
And on the trampoline of life
I'll be bouncing high!

FREE BALLOONS

I gave away my free balloons
And now I haven't any.
It seems I've found the one thing worse
Than having one too many!

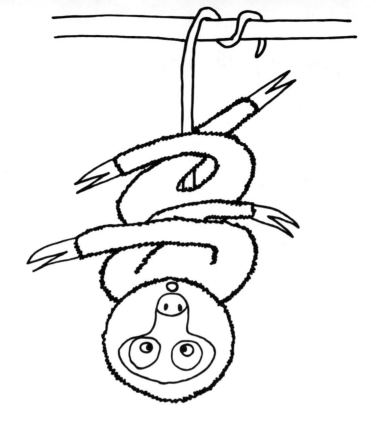

THE MUTANT TWO-TOED SLOTH LEARNS TO COUNT

One was easy, so was two.
Each toe he had gave him a clue.
A paw was free, then he counted to three.
With five toes and a tail he clung to the tree.
His head hung down when he counted to four
But with toed back feet he could do more.
On one of them he counted five and six!
He impressed his friends with mathematical tricks.
In the back of his mind a voice said, "Wait!"
But he bravely went on to seven and eight.
Survival instincts did not yet fail.
From the highest limb he still hung by his tail.
If he'd have stopped there he would have been fine
But the two-toed sloth counted to nine.

FISHIN' OMISSION

Fishing at the summer's dawn
I walk down to the brook,
But have to trudge back home again
'Cause I forgot the hook!
Fishing in the summer morn
And everything's just fine,
But once again I have to leave
'Cause I forgot the line!
Fishing in the afternoon,
A time to rest my soul,
But no rest for the weary here
'Cause I forgot the pole!
Fishing in the evening,
No cause to raise a hackle,
But still I cannot wet my line
'Cause I forgot the tackle!
A summer's day has come and gone
But now I know my wish:
To have another day like this
But just forget to fish!

PICO THE PIGMY

Pico the pygmy is a short little dude
But not in his manners is he ever rude.
He holds open doors for the big and the small
And never makes jokes about folks who are tall.
He welcomes the fat and shakes hands with the thin.
He opens his heart and lets everyone in.
And I wonder how Pico, at just two foot and nine,
Has a heart that's so full, and much bigger than mine.

PEANUT BUTTER PETE:
THE DUEL WITH GRILL CHEESE CHARLIE

Like peanut butter on a summer's day
The rumors had been spreading
That there was going to be a duel
With Grill Cheese Charlie heading
From Kansas down to Texas way
To have it out with PBJ.
Said Charlie, "I won't be retreating
With notches on my belt from eating
Grill cheese on everything I eat
And I'm gonna duel ol' PB Pete."
It came across the telegraph
But Pete dismissed it with a laugh.
"I've eaten cheese. I know the taste.
A shame that bread must go to waste.
Bring him on! I say 'Fine!'
He eats his and I'll eat mine!"
They met upon Enchanted Rock
And each man brought a giant crock
Filled with his own sandwich feast.
(I'd say two hundred each, at least!)
All the folks came out from town
As they stared each other down.
They started eating right at noon
In heat that made the crowd all swoon.

Charlie opened with two in each hand
But Pete would not be thus out-manned.
He gulped and swallowed, burped and spat
And downed ten in just a minute flat.
But Charlie kept on sliding cheddar.
(It went down smoother, being wetter.)
He caught PB Pete at seventeen
But like old cheese was turning green.
He gobbled two, and then three more
Before he passed out on the floor.
Pete calmly ate to twenty-three.
Said, "Folks, that's been enough for me.
There are sandwiches for all who gather,
PB or cheddar if you'd rather.
Charlie's been a noble foe.
Hey! Help me turn him over slow."
And Charlie, (when he got some air),
Said, "Pete, you beat me fair and square!
And in spite of all this dueling fuss
There's a place for both of us."
So between the cheese and peanut butter
They made a pledge to one anudder:
No more duels with food or drink!
A wise move on their part, I think.
Now do like them and be a winner.
Don't talk back! Just eat your dinner!

BOTTOM OF THE TROUGH

I had a dream last night.
This time I was a frog
But I wasn't swimming in a swamp
Or playing in a bog.
It seemed that my perspective
Was just a little off
As I found myself looking up
From the bottom of a trough.
And looking down from high above
With the backdrop of the sky
Was the biggest horse I've ever seen
Who stared me eye to eye.

"Little frog," he said to me,
"I see you've reached a low
And I wonder if you've thought about
Which way you ought to go.
You can scoot along the bottom
And stride from side to side,
But the bottom of the trough
Is a poor sad place to hide.
The only place to go is up.
All you have to do is kick!
And I don't want to gulp a frog
When I lean in for a lick."
So I leapt out of the trough
And woke up in my bed
And remember, when I'm feeling down,
What that wise horse had said.
For just as in my dream
We have times of fear and doubt,
But also the ability
To look up and leap right out!

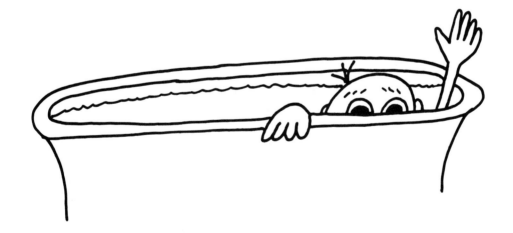

OUR LLAMAS ARE NOT CAMELS

"What can these llamas do?" I asked,
"I'm taking an exotic trip.
I need one to carry burdens
And one who's feet don't slip."
The salesman scratched his chin and said,
"Sir, all our llamas have special gifts.
This one's climbed the highest peaks
And three times his weight he lifts."
"Yes, that's all so well and good," I said,
"But for this trip I need something more.
Can these llamas go without water
For a week on the desert floor?"
The salesman scratched his head a bit,
Then looked deep into my eyes.
"Sir," he said, "I won't say they can
For I do not trade in lies."

OUR HERO

"Our llamas are not camels sir,
Though for llamas they're built well,
But if you need a camel,
I don't have a one to sell."
Our llamas are built for mountain trails,
Not deserts, don't you see?
Would you take your special gift
And then find something else to be?
You're like a llama in the desert
When you misuse that gift of yours,
For a llama's only like a camel
In that it spits a lot and snores!"

THE EARTHWORMS

As I went jogging along the street
I looked down from the sun to my feet.
I saw an earthworm writhing in the heat
And all down the block the same scene repeat.
I stopped my hurried jogging pass,
Started tossing earthworms on the grass.
I picked them up one by one,
Saved them from the scorching sun.
My neighbor said from his lawn chair,
"Friend, what are you doing there?"
"Saving earthworms," was my reply,
"On the pavement they'll dry out and die."
My neighbor looked both left and right,
Said "Friend, try as you might,
You can't possibly save all these earthworms today
And what difference would it make anyway?"
I paused and looked into my neighbor's eyes.
Said "Neighbor, here's what you need to realize:
It made a difference to that —"

100

SPLAT!
My neighbor squashed the earthworm flat!
He smashed another with his shoe,
Said, "Friend, there's something wrong with you.
I think you'd better go inside.
It's hot out here and your brain is fried!"

KNOCKING ON PIPES

The woodpecker is loud today.
It's knocking on pipes again!
Why can't it stick to trees?
That's what the bugs are in!
It sure makes a ruckus,
Attracting my attention.
That pounding gives me headaches,
Migraines, and hypertension.
It does this every day!
It's just too much to bear.
And I can't escape it!
The sound goes everywhere.
And I wonder why it does that
For there is naught to gain.
It simply says, "I'm here!"
From the noise, that much is plain!
And as I sit and write these words,
Bits of poetry,
I start to realize
They are the pipes for me.

ODD THE OTTER

Odd the Otter celebrates Christmas every day.
"That's why we call him Odd," the other otters say.
"He's too small to be a reindeer, too short to be an elf,
But he wears a suit and cap like Santa Claus himself!
There's something so unusual about an otter in those clothes,
But we must admit he brings good cheer everywhere he goes!"
Odd the Otter's secret about the Christmas season
Is to share and give and never need a reason.
And it doesn't take a bright red suit or a ride in Santa's sleigh
To let the love flow from your heart each and every day.

103

AN APOLOGY TO CAMELS

It has been pointed out to me
That I've maligned the camel.
To be sure it's not intentional
For it's such a noble mammal.
But, I see that I have erred,
Been badly in the wrong,
And to make it up to them
I'll sing the camel song:

I went riding on a camel
Into the desert sands!
The camel took me safely
Through these barren lands.
A fortnight without water!
I know! I did the math,
And my camel smells just fine
'Cause I haven't had a bath!

My camel is a friendly sort
To carry me around.
It's succeeded just three times
To throw me to the ground!
But it really is the social type;
It shares its friends with me.
There's only one big problem:
Its best friend is a flea!

I am proud of my nice camel.
It is my one true friend!
It helped me write this song
And gave it a good end.
For I had gone to thank it,
Bent over for some grass,
Then that nasty camel
Bit me on the...DON'T ASK!

BUT—now I can't sit down!
No, you may not have a look!
Don't let your mother read this song
Or she'll throw away my book!

Our llamas are not camels. THANK GOD!

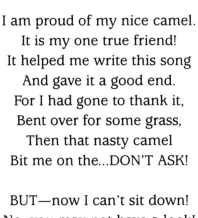

OLLIE, THE
BOBBLEHEAD BOY
48 PIECES

MARK THE MOSQUITO

Mark the Mosquito was a terrible pest.
She sucked blood from people and dogs with such zest!
(Yes, Mark is a boy's name but mosquitos are girls.
In the picture I drew her hair's up in curls.)
She bit a poor duck and a black and white cow.
She would have bitten a llama but couldn't figure out how.
She bit into me asleep in my dreams,
Her hunger too big for a small bug, it seems.
She got bigger and bigger with her grizzly load.
(It's a wonder that Mark did not explode!)
I awoke and I saw her and somehow she flew
But she didn't get far for all the blood that she drew.
It's such a sad story with an ending so dark…

Like the spot on my wall that used to be Mark.

LLAMA-MAN

He was born with the face of a llama
(One only a mother could love)
And his skin grew so leathery
It felt just like a glove.
He has all the powers of the llama!
He is nimble on his feet
And he can live on grass
When that's all there is to eat.
He can climb the tallest mountains
And breathe the thinnest air.
He can carry several hundred pounds
And never really care.
He is always kind and helpful
Anywhere he goes,
But there is always someone
Who makes fun of his big nose.
Oh, it seems so funny
To laugh at other's features
For people can be the kindest
Or the cruelest of all creatures.
So be careful who you ridicule
Lest you should make a gaffe
And yes, you'll know you've stepped in it
When you hear the llama's laugh.

MY PET POSSUM

My eyes surmise it's not so wise
    To play dead like my opossum,
So don't make your abode in the road like a possum or toad
    'Cause I often run across 'em!

THE PATHS DIVIDE

You join us on our journey;
We greet you with a smile.
It's good to have someone like you
Walk with us a while.
You listen while we tell you things
That on our path we've learned.
We watch and marvel at your skill
And the honors you have earned.
Such a pleasant journey
And we wish it would not end,
But we can see our paths divide
As we come around the bend.
There are those who'll tell you
That from our path you must not stray,
But it is your path you walk
And it simply leads away.

But before we reach that junction
There is something we must do:
As your parents we just want to say
How much we think of you.
So hold our hands and talk with us
As we travel side by side.
We promise that we'll let you go
When the paths we take divide.
For somewhere on the road ahead
Our trails will once more touch,
And we'll say then as we do now,
"We love you, so very much."

LEADING THE UNICORN

Free and wild, so beautiful,
The unicorn fills my dreams.
What joy 'twould be to catch it!
So close I am it seems.
And then it walks right up to me!
The reins are in my hands.
Its freedom and its faith are mine
As in front of me it stands.
With such power I am now endowed
To lead it through the land,
But the dream that is the unicorn
I do not understand.

For no matter how I try to lead
I cannot avoid its horn,
And I cannot lead my dreams
Anymore than this unicorn.
What then to do with this magic horse
That gave itself to me?
I take the bridle from its mouth
And let my dreams run free!
I touch the mystic horse of dreams
And its strength I feel inside.
I am one now with my unicorn
And where I go, I ride!

FIDDLE-DEE-DO

Fiddle-de-do, Fiddle-de-dee,
Oh, if you could only see
All the things that trouble me
You could not ignore my plea
And at my side you'd quickly be.

Fiddle-de-dee, Fiddle-de-do,
Even though the rent is due
And the dollars are, well, far too few.
I don't have to tell a friend like you.
You've run away! I guess you knew.

A BAT IN THE BAGPIPES

"Sir Scotsman, please! I'm not a person who gripes
But those shrill shrieks you make mean there's a bat in your pipes.
It's at the high end of the scale of that ol treble cleft
Or so I remember before I went deaf!
Sir, won't you pull that poor bat from the sack
Since there's a ten percent chance I'll get my faculties back!"

"Sir, I must say you are very polite.
Please bear with my bagpipes 'til I get them right.
Don't confuse this high squeaking with the tones of a bat.
Their pitch is quite sharp while I'm playing flat.
But I will reach in and check with a squeeze.
Hey! That was a good one! It brought the crowd to its knees!"

They play them at funerals in a dirge that's so sad
So the dead person's enemies will also feel bad!
They can play them at mine (I'll be safe in the grave)
But you'd better hide like a bat in a cave.
If you can't do that you'd best run away
And cover your ears so the bagpipes can play!

A BUCKET OF SAND

A plastic shovel, two tiny hands,
A bucket filled with shells and sands.
The seagulls call, the child distract
But fly away when they're attacked.
Tiny footprints, that way, this,
The salty breeze, the ocean's kiss.
Memories of bygone days
Return to me with twilight's gaze.
Youth that did the ocean brave
Lost just like the fallen wave
And yet returning to the sea
There's a child who looks like me.
What magic in that tiny hand
That puts time into this pail of sand!

SANDALS

Easy on my feet,
Keep off sand that's hot.
Whenever it is warm
I wear mine a lot.
Sandals make toes happy
'Cause they can wiggle free.
Whenever I wear sandals
So can the rest of me.
No other kind of footwear
Can hold up any candles
To how I feel inside
Whenever I wear sandals.

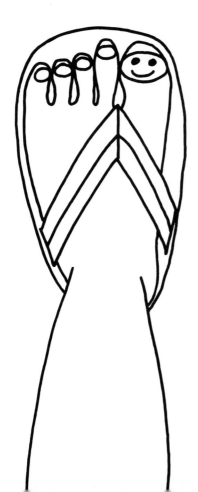
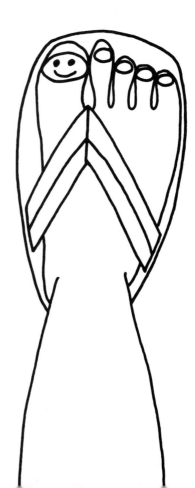

STUBBLE

White hair on my cheek,
Blacker on my chin,
Thicker than on top
Where it's become quite thin.
Wear it on the weekend,
Shave it Monday morn.
Have to go to work
All neat and newly shorn.
I suppose if I forgot
They'd think I was in trouble
But don't suppose I'm not
Just because I don't have stubble.

JIM STEMMLER'S CREDIT CARD

He left it there one Thursday morn,
A noble goodwill gesture.
Breakfast only, so he thought,
Not personal divesture.
Yes, he left it with his friends
But all of them have needs.
Each one wrote a thank you note
To Jim for his good deeds.
He paid for their vacations
To Brazil and Tijuana.
He paid their doctor bills
And bought a pet iguana.
He rented them a luxury box
To watch the Cardinals win,
But when he tried to enter
They wouldn't let him in.
He didn't have his credit card
And his cash was running low,
And, Jim, there's something we must say
That you just have to know.
The credit that you used to have
The bank says you now lack,
And your card has hit the limit
So you can have it back.

119

RAIN ON CANVAS

Rain on canvas comforts me
even though I'm wet.
It conjures up old feelings
that I never will forget.
For I remember days like this
when I went out to camp
and how our friendships grew
despite the cold and damp.
Someone made a fire
and sang a happy song
and with such company
nights didn't seem so long.

I heard the drumbeat playing
on my shelter's canvas roof
and a little on my sleeping bag
for it wasn't waterproof.
We talked the whole night through
right up to the dawn
and like our days of youth
the rain was quickly gone.
But I remember noises
that carry to this day
and the sound of rain on canvas
still takes me far away.

CHASE IT LIKE A SEAGULL

Gliding o'er the waters
Their voices call to me.
Oh, to be a seagull
And fly about, so free!
I'd soar into the dawn
And try to wake the sun
But first I'd strive to reach the stars
And eat them one by one!
If not, it wouldn't matter;
The sea has lots of fish.
To be fat and full and happy,
That's a seagull's wish!

And when the day is over
And the sun has passed on by,
I'd make a final charge
Into the fading sky.
For life is lived but once,
It offers no repeats,
So chase it like a seagull
As the evening sun retreats.
For when the night has fallen
And all the light is gone,
Even in the darkness
Your spirit still flies on.

LAST CHANCE FOR THE BIG PURPLE DOG

"Today's the day." "She needs a home."
The officers' tones were grim
For they'd come to love that purple dog
And she in turn loved them.

But who would take a purple dog?
With such color it can't be well.
And can purple dogs be vicious?
At that time no one could tell.
Time had all run out
And no one took her yet
And the officer hung his head
As he got the phone to call the vet.
"I have a purple dog," he said,
"I'll bring her over in the van."
"Oh good!" said the happy vet,
"For I know a purple man."
It isn't always obvious
Like one's furry coated hue
But everyone needs a special friend
And there is one for you!

STUBBING MY TOE

I kicked a box and stubbed my toe
And now I'm watching where I go.
I'm walking very gingerly.
Does my toe control the rest of me?
It made me hop and made me yell
But what I said I'll never tell!
The only thing I didn't do
Was move the box or wear a shoe,
For that would so defy convention,
Instead of cure to try prevention!

TIME ON MY HANDS

Here's another nonsensical rhyme
About a cuckoo that ate the time.
Both hands it swallowed before it was done
Thinking that would stop the sun.
But the sun kept sinking really fast
Because the hands of time had passed.

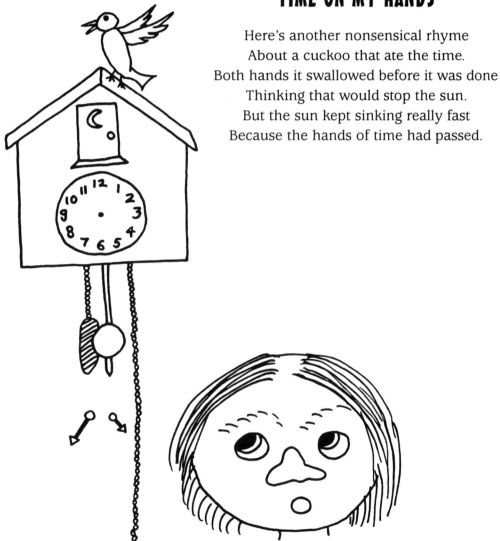

THE LEGEND OF LARRY THE LLAMA

Larry is a little llama,
The soft plush kind, you know.
His eyes are black as coal
And his coat as white as snow.
He sits up on the rail
And the baby grabs his nose,
Hugs him tight and takes him
To Dreamland. There he goes!
It's good to have a llama
In dreams to keep you warm,
And protect you from a nightmare
For Larry can transform.
He can be a horse
To take you safe away
Or take on human likeness
If you need a friend to play.
He can grow some feathers
And be an eagle who can fly,

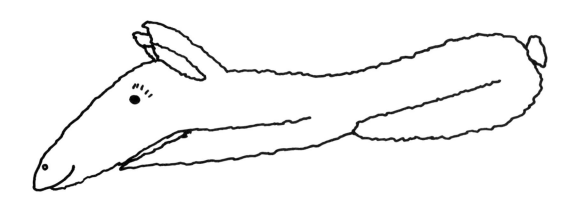

Or even be a unicorn
And touch the stars up in the sky!
Yes, he can take you places
You never thought you'd go,
A friend to stay beside you
As your dreams and body grow.
For Larry is a creature
Of your parents' love
As you are, my darling,
The child we both dreamed of.
And as you ride away with Larry
To that far-off Dreamland hill
May he whisper, "Child, we love you!"
For indeed, we always will.

SAILING UPSIDE DOWN

I was on a boat this morning,
A sailboat in the sea,
But a wave came crashing down
And set it on top of me.
And I have spent these hours
Focusing down under
Into a world I did not know,
And how it makes me wonder
What other worlds there are
That I am unaware of,
Not just under water
But on the land above.

Names and people I don't know
With customs unappealing,
Much as I appear to them
As my vision's now revealing.
And it might be good to spend some time
Underwater watching fish
Or walking in another's shoes —
Perhaps that's too big a wish.

LIFE SKILLS...AND SPILLS!

Glue and paint in big flat pans
Right beside the soda cans!
Mixed together nice and thick,
Don't drink it now or you'll get sick!
It won't stick to paper now
But face and shirt and hands — and how!
My leader says, "To learn life skills
We will have our little spills."
I guess that's why at summer camp
They don't mind if I go home damp.
They just look at me and say,
"I hope your Mom's on time today!"

THAT'S OUR TRAIN!

We counted cars, one-thirty five!
That's the longest train alive!
Hey, we're stopped now at the light.
Count again! Make sure we're right.
We're passing it! Let's count once more.
That makes three times. Let's do four!
But my mother who was driving us
Said, "If you do, you'll take the bus!"

SQUEAKY BRAKES

My car has squeaky brakes
And a nasty engine pop.
Will it ever start again?
I don't know, 'cause I CAN'T STOP!

THUMB KIND OF CARPENTER

Oh, yes! I am proud
Of this fine craft I made.
It made me quite familiar
With the nurses at first aid.
Yes, I'm personally acquainted
With nails and hammer hits.
My counselor said to hammer
I should wear oven mitts!
But I don't' think it's fair.
It's stupid and it's dumb!
But I'm sure I would think differently
If my brain were in my thumb!
My dad said to try harder.
He'd help me if he could.
He held the nail for me
'Til I smacked him pretty good.
I saw the tears well up.
Said, "Father, please don't cry!
You taught me not to quit
So I'll give it one more try!"
My father shook his head
And hid his thumb from me.
Said, "Son, please don't give up.
Just find something else to be!"

SNEEZIN' SAM

It first it was a sniffle
And a twitching, itching nose
From a little bit of dust
Or a cat hair I suppose.
He took a breath, blinked his eyes
And readied for a sneeze
But in spite of his contortions
It was just a tease.
His nostrils flared and widened
And got bigger than his eyes.
He inhaled again and doubled
Then quadrupled them in size!

Like a giant vacuum
He sucked up all the dust,
Some paper clips, rubber bands,
The cat (Oh, how she fussed!),
A couple of lamps, five books
And a full screen TV.
(How he did that is still
A mystery to me!)
Then quick as it started
It stopped again.
Sam didn't sneeze
So it all stayed in.
If such a thing had occurred to me
It would have bothered me a lot
But Sam's sinuses were cavernous
So eventually, he forgot.
His nose returned to normal size.
His nostrils didn't swell.
For a year or so he carried on
And got around quite well.
Everyone who knew him
Thought that Sam was cured
Until one day, unexpectedly,
A tragedy occurred.
SAM SNEEZED!

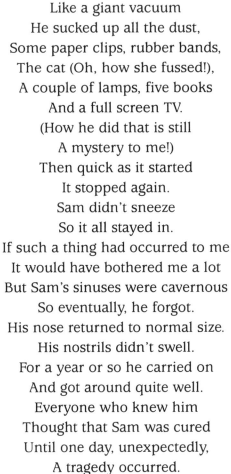

The dust the paper clips
rubber bands a disheveled cat
the lamps the books and yes the TV
suddenly
SQUEEZED
out Sam's normal sized schnoz
(which they later packed with ice and with gauze)
And from that day to this
No matter how sick that I am
I'm glad I'm not Sam.

BILL'S FRIENDS

Bill's friends were many
When Bill's bills were few
But disappeared quickly
Like the cash he withdrew.
It's in difficult times
We find out who's true
And that's why I want
A friend just like you.

BILLS   FRIENDS   (BILL)

NEANDERTHAL NELL AND ME

Nell the Neanderthal lived in a cave.
(To do that today would be daring and brave!)
She didn't have lights by which she could read.
(There weren't any books so there was no need.)
But scientists say she had shoes for her feet
And berries and roots and game she could eat.
She had fire and furs to protect from the cold
But Nell lived in an age when thirty was old.
For a Neanderthal gal she did pretty well
But I want to live in a house, not a cave like poor Nell.
So if I gave you a laugh, PLEASE find someone to tell
That Byron the poet has a good book to sell!

MY SUIT OF ARMOR

I'm locked up inside it.
If there's fear I can hide it.
My suit of armor is clean and shiny.
I wasn't sure when I tried it
Yet now I confide it
Protects my hide and my heinie.
But I sweat in the sun
And it's too heavy to run.
There's no way I can move about.
So like a statue I stand.
Oh no! I've been canned!
Could someone please let me out?

IVAR AND THE SEAGULLS

They wonder at the gentleman
With beard and hair so white
Who walks out on the farthest pier
To feed the gulls tonight.
They tell him it's a waste of time.
The seagulls don't need him.
He chuckles and replies he knows
But he sure does need them.
They follow him in confidence
He won't run out of bread.
Not anxious or contentious,
They trust his love instead.

And I wonder as I watch them
Circling above
If the seagulls are so gentle
Because of Ivar's love.
He doesn't judge or label them.
He enjoys their company.
There's no charge for this affection.
Like the bread, it's offered free.
And I pray that there are people
Who watch with me today
And learn from Ivar and the seagulls
How to give their love away.

PAUSE TO DREAM

As I wandered
down a path
I came upon a stream
and there I sat
to rest,
to ponder,
and to dream.
I listened to
the birds
(a gentle breeze
was blowing)
and thought about
important things
like where my life
was going.
Which way would
I be walking
if I were following
my heart?
And when better than
today
would be
the time to start?
And I watched
the water
wash away
leaves fallen
yesterday
and decided
it was best
to begin without
delay.

A DIFFERENT PATH

I wandered down
a brand new path
that led
I know not where
and wondered
would I know the end
if ever I got there.
Each turn,
each twist,
each step I took
led me somewhere
new
and there were places
grown so thick
that I could scarce get through.
And when I paused
to look
and plan my next
attack
I could hear
the voices
calling to
come back.
Swiftly then
I'd lift my feet
and quickly stride
ahead,
away from
old mistakes
to new mysteries
instead.

So I stood
and stretched,
and shook my head,
and looked around
once more,
picked up my things
and chose a path
different
than before.

And then
the voices
faded,
my narrow trail
grew wide,
and suddenly
I felt my heart
as it beat
with joy
inside.

NOT SHAKESPEARE

You're not Shakespeare or Mark Twain.
You're not Shel or Dr. Seuss.
Your fables aren't like Aesop's
Or even Mother Goose!
Who do you think you are
To write in such a way?
You haven't suffered quite enough.
You've still got dues to pay!
The people smile and tell you
That you have talent, sure,
But when it comes to buying
They almost all demure.
You'd better keep your day job
'Cause on this you can't subsist
And all the stories have been told.
There's not a one they've missed.

No, I am not Shakespeare
And I never was Mark Twain
But I have paid my dues in full
And had my share of pain.
Dr. Seuss is long since gone
And I no longer hear from Shel
But after Goose and Aesop
There still are tales to tell.
With my pencil and my paper
I'll give it my best try
And I guess if you are reading this
I succeeded, didn't I?
But I don't need a reason
To do this thing I do
'Cause I like to tell my stories
To folks I like, like you!

THE END OF THE
BOOK

Don't stop to look!
This is the end of the book.
The fables and stories are through,
Though there's a theory that
There's a very white bat
But how can we tell if it's true?
For how would you find
A bat of that kind?
These pages would hide an albino.
Yet there's a rumor I've heard
(I think it's absurd)
That there's also a giant white rhino.
It has a perfect disguise
'Til it opens its eyes.
It runs in a great cloud of dust.
If you see that I suppose
This book you will close
For if you value your life, you must.

But even things strange
Like a rhino can change
As life takes them through joy and sorrow.
And if this book that you read
Put new thoughts in your head
I hope you'll read it again tomorrow!

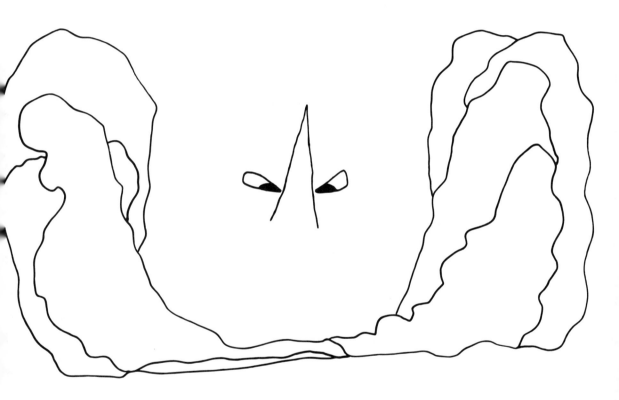

Thanks

The one person without whom this book would never have been published and who did absolutely the most work on it is my wife, Sharon. You made the book complete and you make my life complete. I love you!

Byron

Author's Notes

I am frequently asked how I came to write a particular poem and while the specifics differ, it's usually from one of a few sources. It's almost always from an inspiration about a title or line and I start writing without knowing the "meaning". I think that's what makes writing so much fun, because writing the poem to find the meaning at the end is kind of like solving a puzzle. Sometimes I get an image from a dream. Other times I watch or listen to people I meet, and sometimes I just sit quietly and listen or watch the things around me. And most of the time, thank God, inspiration comes.

I'm going to tell you about several of the poems in the book and how I came to write them. If I miss your favorite poem and you'd like to hear about it, you can e mail me through my website at www.byronvonrosenberg.com or just type "I don't want to kiss a llama" into the search box and my website will show up as one of the first choices. Which leads me into my first story . . .

I had been trying to write poems about llamas but wasn't happy with any of them. (We had visited an exotic animal farm and were intrigued by how intelligent and cute the llamas were.) One morning as I was starting to wake, I heard a voice in a dream shout out, "Our llamas are not camels!" and I awoke suddenly. By the end of the day, I had written the poem and even got my wife to like it (not always a given for my favorite poems). She liked it so much that she got on the internet and ordered a stuffed toy llama. Later, just horsing (or is that llama-ing?) around, I held it up to my daughter and said, "Erin, kiss the llama!" She scoffingly replied, "I don't want to kiss a llama!" (instead of her usual, "Dad, you're scaring me!") and I had to write the poem right away. After some "help" from Sharon, that poem was written and became the book by the same name which, incidentally, is how I came to draw the pictures which led to my drawing pictures for this book and blah, blah, blah. Now you know why I write poetry! I'm just so long winded otherwise!

"Thinking Upside Down" had a somewhat similar beginning as I lay on my old couch downstairs in the basement. I was trying to think of something wonderful to write and not having much success. I picked up my head to look around the room for something to inspire me and, finding nothing (you should see the mess in our basement!), laid my head back down and closed my eyes. And for an instant, I felt like I was dizzy or upside down. Well, the title came to me and I had to write the poem. I think Sharon approved it without any changes!

Lately I've come to realize that I was in the Bat Patrol in Boy Scouts as a boy. (I was in Troop 48 in New Orleans, Louisiana.) We always tried to be the best patrol and hollered our patrol name every time we won an event. Something there may have stuck, since I've counted some four or five poems that involve the flying rodents in this book alone! And I still have the old bat patrol flag we made. (This is really weird. As Erin would say, "Dad, you're scaring me!")

And it continues! My brother Gene is Scoutmaster of the troop and my son, Ryan, just got his Eagle Scout award this year!

"Leap from Your Dreams" is another morning dream poem which I wrote in June, 2004 at my mother's house in Georgetown, Texas. I had one of those dreams where it takes forever to get somewhere and, as I started to get up, realized I didn't have time to "return" from my dream. Since I had to get up and take the kids to camp, I remember thinking I'd have to "leap" from my dream. I didn't leap that fast; I wrote the whole poem before I woke anyone up. I had to go into town for a photo at the paper and I corrected my mistakes while I waited for the photographer. Then I read the poem to the local Kiwanis Club just a few hours after I wrote it! I used the four animals, I guess because it reminded me so of the "I Don't Want to Kiss a Llama!" poem. ("I Don't Want to Kiss a Llama!" is not in this book, but it is in *Climb the Red Mountain* and, obviously, in *I Don't Want to Kiss a Llama!*)

I wrote "An Apology to Camels" when I was contacted by attorneys from the camel lobby threatening to sue me because I had treated the camel poorly *vis a vie* the llama. It's a really nice apology, isn't it?

I'm going to jump around a bit (you might have figured that out already) because I think it'll be more fun than going through the book poem by poem in order. I don't remember what inspired the first poem "Free Balloons" (probably a balloon give-away at the bank or a mall), but I drew the picture for it in February of 2005 as I began preparing this book. I made a pun (I make lots of those as you can see) with the numbers on the balloon 1-2-MANY, and put it in the book. Then just a few days ago, I saw some balloons outside the office where I work. I had wanted to follow up with a second verse, but nothing had come to mind until then. And without remembering the picture consciously, I thought of "any" and rhymed it with "many" and there you go! I find it amazing how the whole thing tied together from such apparently disconnected parts. Kind of makes you think there's a bigger plan out there, doesn't it?

And there's more! For "The Trampoline of Life" (inspired by the trampoline at my brother's house) I had already placed the balloon girl in the picture but I had told Sharon I wanted to take it out. But I needed a happy way for the balloon girl to land, so I drew a trampoline in the second "Free Balloons" poem. That had to be after the trampoline poem, I thought, and when I turned to that picture, there was my balloon girl already floating above the trampoline in the picture drawn months earlier. (I kind of like to think someone's watching out for me like that in case I give away all my free balloons. And I believe someone is doing the same for you!)

"Alonzo the Tinkerer" was inspired by my maternal grandfather, Alonzo Taylor, who did actually like to tinker with his watches and clocks. Sometimes he even got them fixed! (It really was amazing; I could never understand those things at all!) The ticks and tocks part was inspired by the really loud ticking of an alarm clock in the basement which I got for helping to raise money for the Muscular Dystrophy Association which I did because my father got ALS which inspired my creative writing through the poem "Look at My Hands" which is the dedication to my first book *Don't Feed the Seagulls*. It makes my head dizzy to write all this! If you are getting confused, remember, this is the Author's Notes and it's supposed to be that way. You bought (or were given) the book for the poems, fables and sketches! As an aside, I should note that one of my cousins said I had my grandfather's sense of humor, to which another replied, "Yeah, but Grandpa's eighty years old. What's Byron's excuse?" (P. S. - I don't have any! And no, I'm not that old yet!)

My granddad also played chess and taught me to play when I was about nine. I like to read "Endgame" because it reminds me of time spent with him. I have another chess poem, "Chess with Grandpa" which is in *Don't Feed the Seagulls*.

We home school and I wrote "The Paths Divide" for my son, Ryan, on the occasion of his eighth grade graduation. (They had the parents come up and say something about the graduates. It went over pretty well and our children all forgave us for the sappy things we said. I think!) It's a different poem from so many in the book that are funny (or attempt to be). If that surprised you, I'm sorry. I hope you liked it anyway and, who knows, it could be somebody's favorite.

One of my wife's favorites (my wife and Sharon are the same person if you haven't figured that out) is "King Louie's Horse's Butt: A Love Story". And no, we didn't really meet that way, but if we'd have met there that's the kind of thing my wife would have said! Actually, I go to Forest Park and write outside, but when it's too cold (a decision that depends on my mood) I go the one of the museums (entry is free!) because it's warm. I don't remember what else I wrote that day, but as I left I looked up and saw, well, the horse's butt. The title came into my mind immediately and as I walked away, it also came to me that it must be a love poem, perhaps to soften the impact of that "bad" word. I called my mother with the first draft and she was adamant that I not read that poem. She did, however, coach me to improve the verses which were, at first, somewhat repetitive and cumbersome. (Yes, even more than they are now. I saw that one coming!) Usually when I write a poem, I go over it again or read it to Sharon and then consider it finished, moving on to the next one quickly. "KLHB" was different, and I worked on it off and on for a week or so. The final version was completed just before I sent the first draft of *Climb the Red Mountain* to the printer several months later. (The poem was first printed in that book.) I used my rhyming dictionary to find all the words rhyming with "butt".

I do take suggestions and do listen although I'm not very good at giving that impression. I had told Sharon that I wanted to use only the picture of the statue for KLHB, ("the poem's good enough on it's own!") but Sharon wanted me to make some more drawings for it. I'm glad she did because I like the mummy!

Taking suggestions is a learned art, and when I was little my older sister Carol and I seemed to always be at odds. Yeah, I argued with my brothers, but Carol could really get my goat and she knew it. When I was fourteen or so, I got so angry one time that I took a swing and was afraid that I hurt her. I was so ashamed and remorseful and scared! I went to her and told her how sorry I was and that I wanted us to be the best of friends for the rest of our lives. I don't think we've spoken a cross word since (yes, we still talk!), but I'm still so ashamed I'm not sure I'm going to put this story in the book. So when a drive past Arnot, Texas inspired "Arnot and Artu, the Llamas from France" it had a real life meaning for me. Please, please, please! No matter how angry or jealous you feel, always love and show love to the people you are closest to, even and especially when they don't or can't. It will make a difference, if not in them, then in you.

Here's another story you might find interesting (as if any of the other ones were!). It has to do with a lack of talent combined with very poor handwriting and poor lighting. When I was in junior high school, my parents "encouraged" us to take up a musical instrument to play in the band. I was going to do the tuba, but I got the impression it might be too expensive (my parents sent us to private school on my father's professor's salary alone) and chose the flute. Unfortunately, my fingers were not so nimble as to play very well at all. So, at concerts and competitions, I turned the flute slightly towards myself and blew but no noise (note choice of word "noise" instead of "music") was made because the air went over the metal, not the hole. (You blow over the opening like you're playing a soda bottle. That's easy. But try moving YOUR fingers that fast!) I must have been good at faking it, because when I told my mother about it last year, she would not believe it. Then she got mad! So I was inspired to write a poem called "The Fraudulent Flutist" and scribbled that title in my notebook. Writing one evening in my son's room (I think he was watching TV in mine) the shades were drawn and I misread my own handwriting as "The Flatulent Flutist". Believe me, I approached that title with some trepidation, but it's really supposed to be funny. It gives Sharon a hoot (you can tell I am old with the use of that phrase) whenever she hears it!

"Prophet the Llama" has an interesting origin. My wife noticed an all black horse with an all white mane near the highway at Bourbon, Missouri when we were on one of our recent trips. She is a person who sees things clearly so I made the connection to a prophet and using a rule of poetry that I recently discovered (that is, if you have a llama in your poem it makes it twice as good!), I changed Prophet into a llama. I wrote that poem three times, never revising, just starting over.

"These Geese Don't Fly on Tuesdays" and "Invasion of the Woodpeckers" were written on the same day in October, 2002 at a campout to Beaumont Scout Reservation near Eureka, Missouri. I just listened to the sounds of nature around me and let my hand go to work. When I write a poem like that, it seems like my hand writes the words before I think them. (Hey, maybe that's why I had to self-publish my book, you think?) Then it's really fun for me to read them. Other poems inspired by visits to the park include "The Squirrels' Quarrel" and "Leading the Unicorn". (Our zoo in St. Louis has some really unique animals. REALLY unique!)

"Climb the Red Mountain" is one of those "serious" poems that was inspired in a similar fashion. There are beautiful hills in Jefferson County, Missouri where I live, and one fall evening the sun turned the whole hillside red. I'm planning a book of poems and praise called *Diamonds of the Dawn* which was inspired by those hills as well. Ever wonder why you ended up in a place at a certain time? There's gotta be a reason!

"Turnabout Mountain" came from looking at a map (You should always leave an atlas in your bathroom, especially if you have a class in geography. Is that TMI?)

and finding a creek named Turnabout. I write more about mountains than creeks possibly because I grew up in New Orleans where the only hill was in Audubon Park . (Monkey Hill is now part of the zoo, probably with real monkeys on it. Come to think of it, it was probably named for the kids who played on it more than its proximity to the zoo!) Anyway, I worte a poem about a mountain, not a creek. I must have been altitude deprived!

I did write a poem about a creek called "Pause to Dream". It runs next to "A Different Path" because I think the two go well together. The picture of the small rock on top of the larger one is a trail sign meaning "this is the trail." Yes, from my old Scout Handbook!

Seasons do play a role in the poems as they do in our lives. "I'm Collecting" was written on January 1, 2005 as an end of the year poem. I have lots of Christmas poems in my other books and in upcoming ones. I may even do a Christmas book, perhaps entitled *Oh Christmas Treed* about my cat's adventures with our tree. (That's a poem from *Red Mountain*.)

Some of the poems were inspired by real life experiences. I was a camp director (name and location of camp not to be mentioned) where they held a breath holding contest every week and had for decades. The one summer I was there, in front of three hundred people, this one boy nearly drowned because he held his breath so long he passed out. And I was the camp director! I remember running all the way up the hill and trying to control my own breath to tell people to call 911, but by the time they understood me, the lad had recovered and asked his now infamous question. I guess I could write another story about the heart attack I nearly had!

"The Dead Snake's Bite" is also about a real life experience at a camp. (Moms, camp is really fun and please send your kids. It's just so much fun to write about the one or two really stupid things that happened. I hope to do a whole book on the wonderful things that happen at camp and have a few of those in my book, *Climb the Red Mountain* as well as in this one. What, you didn't read "Thumb Kind of Carpenter", "Life Skills . . . and Spills!", "Our Train", or "Rain on Canvas"? Some of them were funny, too!) For "The Dead Snake's Bite" there isn't that much imagination involved; that's pretty much the way it happened. I wasn't involved in that camp, but heard about it later and helped with some of the paperwork. Strangely enough, the insurance company didn't have a category for "dead snake's bite"!

I wrote "Sneezin' Sam" because I just had to sneeze but didn't. The picture looks something like a friend of mine named Sam, but I'm not giving out any last names. (Not yet at least. But read on. . .) Hey, you know who you are!

No, I never knew "The Little Pyromaniac" but a lot of other people have! I read that poem and it seems like someone is always telling me about the time somebody blew up the outhouse! Think there might be a lesson here?

I know lots of teachers and they do inspire. The students at the Our Lady Queen of Peace elementary school in House Springs, Missouri, encouraged me to write about their teachers and lo and behold, "My Teacher Is a Treasure" was written shortly thereafter. Does that sound like your teacher? Maybe "The Gingerbread Man Gets a Haircut" is more his or her style. Or yours! And maybe you had an English teacher like "Thesaurosaurus"! That one was inspired by Ryan's love of dinosaurs and the book I carry around along with my rhyming dictionary.

Some of my poems come from a combination of real life and imagination. "Gene Cleans" is one of those that happened recently. Gene maintains the building where I work and we have a set of glass doors that open to the street. The weather had recently changed from rainy to sunny and Gene was cleaning the glass as he often does. I joked about his wiping the clouds away and he remarked that I shouldn't wash my car unless I wanted the rain to come back. I think I composed that poem almost entirely in my head. It must have struck my imagination in a special way.

"Telepathic Tina" followed Gene on the same day because I read that poem to Tina who was working our switchboard. She wanted a poem about her and I paused to think. Just then a call came and the caller asked Tina if a particular person was in. Tina responded politely and connected the call. Then she wondered aloud, "How do they think I know that?" Imagination and alliteration took it from there. So if you have a neat idea or experience or know a really interesting person, maybe I can write a poem about them. Or better yet, you do it!

Walter Wupperman never knew he'd get a poem written about him. As a matter of fact, it was his younger brother, Alfred, who really made that fateful trip down the hill on Texas Street. They were my father's cousins and they all grew up in the same neighborhood in Austin, Texas. I remember another cousin of his, Dick Schenck, telling me the story following my father's memorial service. (I had only just begun to write these poems with one I wrote for my dad the week before. Called "Look at My Hands," it's on my website at www.byronvonrosenberg.com and in *Don't Feed the Seagulls*.) By the time I got home, I had forgotten which Wupperman the story was about and just liked the way "Walter Wupperman's Wings" sounded so much better. My uncle, Charles von Rosenberg, assures me that Walter would "roll over in his grave" to be put in that story, so this paragraph is my effort to undo that harm.

There is a real person named Jim Stemmler and even though he's a lawyer, he agreed to let me put him in the book. He is a member of the Optimist Club I joined in 2003 and I like him a lot, perhaps because he has a sense of humor like mine! The club is a lot of fun and they meet on Thursday mornings at the Schlafly Library in St. Louis. Jim is a charter member (he was there back in 1962 when they started the club) and headed the nominating committee that asked me to be president next year. Things have really hit rock bottom for our club! (But drop by if you want to hear one of my latest poems!)

"Come Out Smiling" was inspired by a visit to another Optimist Club. (Optimist Clubs do things to help youth grow up happy and well and they have fun.) Uncle Russ really liked one of my unpublished poems about a cat, so I wrote it out for him in his book. We visited a bit and he reminded me of my grandfather, Alonzo.

There was also a real person named Ivar but I did not know him. I visited Seattle for one day in 2004 on the way back from Alaska and ate at a restaurant named Ivar's. I saw an elderly gentleman feeding the seagulls from the dock. Later, I noticed a nearby statue of Ivar, the late owner of the establishment, and guess what he was doing? You got it! Feeding the seagulls. (In case you missed it from the back of the book, my first book of poems is called *Don't Feed the Seagulls!*) Now remember, I was only there one night, and (I didn't tell you this) just drove downtown at the suggestion of the hotel clerk. I got so confused in all the traffic that I had decided to go back to the hotel without stopping but then I finally saw a parking space. I walked a couple of blocks to the water and arrived immediately at Ivar's. I had no idea he liked seagulls and never had heard of his restaurant before. And as creative as some people think I am, I'm not crazy enough to think that anyone would believe that story if I made it up!

I do love seagulls and the beach, so I'm always looking for a new poem to write about those subjects. (Did I tell you that my first book is titled *Don't Feed the Seagulls*? Oh, yeah. Last paragraph. Sorry!) If I lived closer to the beach, that might be all I wrote about ("A Bucket of Sand", "Chase It Like a Seagull", "Sandals"). We used to live in Corpus Christi, Texas and still have dear friends who live there. It's always so relaxing to go to the beach and it was especially nice to be so close when the children were small. We almost bought a home on the island and stayed and sometimes I wish we did, especially with prices going up so much!

Now, I gotta tell you about "Ollie, the Bobble Head Boy". I'll be honest and tell you that I was semi-awake (a rather constant state as those who know me best will attest) and saw a bobble head boy turn and look at me. (Sometimes these images appear on the inside of my eyelids. Must have been that cataract surgery. I'll have to talk to the ophthalmologist!!) He (Ollie, not the ophthalmologist) had food on his face, so obviously he was alive. And you can figure out how the rest of the story was inspired. (Hello, Pinnochio!) I just wrote a poem yesterday called "Rollie the Collie, the Bobble Head Dog" which will have to be in my next book. I don't have a title for that book yet, but I am writing poems. Writing poems is like "Squeaky Brakes" (inspired the same day as "Free Balloons") — I can't stop!

(Okay, it's a week later and I have a title poem to use for the next book. Trouble is, I can't decide which title would be better. I started with one but kind of like the other one. Do you like *Stars to Chase* or *My Place in Space* better? E-mail me through the website at www.byronvonrosenberg.com and let me know!)

I also saw "Neanderthal Nell" in a dream (now there's a really scary thought!) but "Ookle McGlookle" was an actual toy we had growing up. I made a cartoon of him back in sixth grade at St. Andrew's Episcopal School in a little newspaper my friend Robert Sims (see, I did put last names in!) and I originated. Maybe this creative writing thing has a longer history than I thought! (I'm sure if I could go back and read it I would be convinced otherwise!)

My wife and daughter saw an otter in Branson, Missouri where I often do book signings at T. Charleston and Sons in the Grand Village and at Madison Books and Print in Silver Dollar City. When they told me about it later, I said that the otter "ought to" be careful in a place with so many people and cars. I liked the sound of it and wrote the poem which I have come to enjoy very much.

I remember my dad (his name was Dale and he had a doctorate from M. I. T. so he was very smart) telling us he wanted us to have fun while we were growing up because we had the rest of our lives to work. Maybe that's what inspired the poem.

Sharon says I have to write about "The Earthworms". It was about a month after my dad had passed away and I was writing every day, but not sure what direction to take this new gift of creative writing. (If you'll read "Leading the Unicorn", you'll realize who is leading whom!) As I looked at all the earthworms on the pavement that morning, it struck me to think of the starfish poem ("It made a difference to that one") and I immediately began a bellylaugh that lasted on and off throughout the day. My dad used to call me with jokes he liked and I couldn't help but think of him as I wrote the poem. I wrote the poem as soon as I got back home and ended up late for work! I followed up with two more earthworm poems which are in the *Seagulls* book..

"Super-Frog" owes its inspiration to "The Earthworms" and to some friends here in Missouri. I read the earthworm poem to Lenora Richter and she suggested I write a poem about the frogs and toads that jump across the road in the springtime, sometimes into the paths of cars. I don't remember why I came up with the idea making the frog a superhero, but it is a really funny poem, I think. Lenora's husband Fred provided the inspiration for "Larry the Llama" by naming the llama (a stuffed one, silly!) we gave to their son Jonathan. Jonathan helped by dragging the llama into his crib!

One quick note: Yes, I know my sloth is not anatomically correct as its toes and tail are different than what you'd normally find, but remember, it's a MUTANT! Like I said, we have really unique animals here in St. Louis. (And people, too! Look more closely at the foot in "Stubbing My Toe.")

Just a couple more and I'll let you go. Oh really, I doubt if anyone will ever read this far anyway. You know, that's the amazing thing about this writing. I never really expected to write anything anyone would want to read. Yeah, I remember the history papers and science projects, but they had to pay the teachers to read those. So if anyone reads any of this book and gets something useful (and I use that term loosely) from it, it's far more than I could have hoped. Thank you for sticking with it and I hope it was worth the time and the trip!

The interaction between our dog Neko, a female rat terrier, and Star, the cat my wife fell in love with and got us to adopt, gave the idea for "Oil and Water." Neko is Ryan's dog and he named her. Her name means "cat" in Japanese. Maybe that's why the dog and cat play so well together.

Neko is, of course, the inspiration for "Ivan the Terrier" which is a name that popped into my head when I was sleeping. (Well obviously I woke up! Duh!) "Treed Off" is about Star again because she loves to look outside but hates to go there. I think she'd knock the door down to get back in before she climbed a tree! Star also likes to "dance" on my chest before she tries to sleep there and so inspired "Dances with Cats", too.

Well, I could go on and on, but I'm getting tired and you're probably ready to finish this and write your book report! (As if your teacher would ever approve such a book for a report. If you're lucky, you've already graduated and are reading this for fun. If not, write a poem in your book report and ask for extra credit.) In any case, I hope you have as much fun reading it as I did writing it, but I think I said that before. And even though I am constantly reminded (thank you, Charlie Nutter) that I am "Not Shakespeare" (I can't believe I spelled that right without spell check!), hopefully you found something of value here.

For you peanut butter lover's, I'm afraid the inspiration for Peanut Butter Pete is and must always remain a mystery. As with Sneezin' Sam, you know who you are!

TTFN!

Byron von Rosenberg
May 10, 2005
Byrnes Mill, Missouri

Alphabetical List of Poems

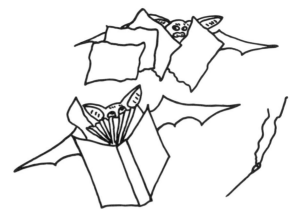

BATS IN THE BINDING

If you are finding some bats in the binding
Please refer your complaints to the printer.
He was paid extra cash to sew and to lash
The paper so bats couldn't enter.
But they're back again! They just keep flying in
Like thoughts leap into my head.
And I hope you can claim your thoughts do the same,
Perhaps from something your read.
For if you fall asleep with thoughts good and deep
It will chase your worries away.
Then with a whisper or shout let those good thoughts out
And tomorrow will be a great day!
As for the bats in the pages, I don't pay any wages.
(They do what they do for free.)
But since they've been loosed I've gotten quite used
To bats — and thoughts! — friendly to me!